DROPSHIPPING FOR BEGINNERS

A Step-by-Step Guide to Starting a Profitable
Online Business

Introduction:

- What drop-shipping is and its growing popularity as a business model
- The benefits and challenges of drop-shipping
- The purpose of the book and what you can expect to learn

Chapter 1: The Basics of Drop-shipping

- How drop-shipping works
- The different types of drop-shipping
- The benefits and drawbacks of drop-shipping

Chapter 2: Finding Profitable Products

- How to research profitable product niches
- How to source products from reliable suppliers
- Examples of profitable products to drop-ship

Chapter 3: Setting Up Your Online Store

- The different options for building an online store, including Shopify and other store builders
- How to set up a Shopify store step-by-step, including themes, product pages, and payment options
- Tips on optimising your store for conversions

Chapter 4: Choosing the Right Wholesalers

- The different types of wholesalers available
- Reliable and profitable drop-ship wholesalers for beginners
- How to evaluate wholesalers

Chapter 5: Marketing Your Business

- How to market your business
- The importance of creating a strong brand identity
- Successful drop-shipping businesses and their marketing strategies

Chapter 6: Managing Your Business

- How to manage your inventory and track sales
- Tips on providing excellent customer service
- How to scale your business and manage growth

Conclusion:

- Key takeaways from the book
- Take action and start your own drop-shipping businesses
- Additional resources for further learning and support

INTRODUCTION

Welcome

In recent years, the rise of e-commerce has transformed the way people shop and do business. With the advent of drop-shipping, entrepreneurs can now start an online business with little to no upfront investment in inventory, and can operate from anywhere in the world. Drop-shipping is a business model where a retailer doesn't hold any physical inventory and instead sources products from third-party suppliers who ship the products directly to the customer.

Drop-shipping has become a popular business model for beginners and experienced entrepreneurs alike, thanks to its low start-up costs and potential for high profits. However, the process of starting a drop-shipping business can be overwhelming for those who are new to e-commerce. It can be challenging to navigate the crowded market and find profitable products, reliable suppliers, and effective marketing strategies.

This book is designed to provide a step-by-step guide for beginners who want to start a drop-shipping business. We will cover the basics of drop-shipping, how to find profitable products and reliable suppliers, how to set up your online store, and how to market and manage your business. By following the strategies and examples provided in this book, you can start a successful drop-shipping business and achieve financial freedom.

Whether you're looking to escape the 9-to-5 rat race or simply want to create a passive income stream, drop-shipping can be an excellent way to achieve your goals. Let's dive into the world of drop-shipping and discover how you can build a profitable online business!

CHAPTER 1: THE BASICS OF DROPSHIPPING

Drop-shipping has become an increasingly popular way for entrepreneurs to start an online business. This retail fulfilment method allows retailers to sell products without actually keeping inventory in stock. Instead, they purchase products from a third-party supplier who then ships the products directly to the customer. In this chapter, we will explore the basics of drop-shipping, including how it works, the different types of drop-shipping, and the benefits and drawbacks of using this model.

How Dropshipping Works

The drop-shipping model works as follows: a retailer sources products from a supplier, who then ships the products directly to the customer. The retailer never actually handles the products themselves, and instead relies on the supplier to fulfil orders.

Here's a step-by-step breakdown of the drop-shipping process:

1. A customer places an order on the retailer's website.
2. The retailer forwards the order details to the supplier.
3. The supplier ships the product directly to the customer.
4. The retailer profits from the difference between the wholesale and retail price.

One of the key advantages of drop-shipping is that it allows retailers to start an online store without needing to invest in inventory upfront. This means that the initial startup costs are significantly lower than traditional e-commerce businesses. Additionally, retailers can easily add or remove products from their store without worrying about managing inventory.

Different Types of Drop-shipping

There are two main types of drop-shipping: <u>domestic</u> drop-shipping and <u>international</u> drop-shipping.

Domestic drop-shipping refers to sourcing products from suppliers within your own country. This has the advantage of faster shipping times, lower shipping costs, and greater control over the quality of the products.

International drop-shipping, on the other hand, involves sourcing products from suppliers overseas. This can offer a wider range of products and lower wholesale prices, but can also result in longer shipping times, higher shipping costs, and potential issues with customs.

For example, let's say you want to start an online store selling fitness equipment. You find a domestic supplier who specialises in workout equipment and offers drop-shipping services. By sourcing your products domestically, you can ensure faster shipping times and a lower risk of issues with customs.

On the other hand, if you want to sell products that are not available in your country, you may need to source products from an international supplier. For example, if you want to sell handcrafted jewellery from Bali, you would need to source products from an international supplier who can ship products directly to your customers.

Benefits of Drop-shipping

The primary advantage of drop-shipping is the low start-up costs. Since retailers do not have to invest in inventory, they can launch their business with minimal upfront costs. Additionally, the drop-shipping model allows retailers to offer a wider variety of products without the risk of overstocking. Other benefits of drop-shipping include:

Other benefits of drop-shipping include:

1. Flexibility: Drop-shipping allows retailers to operate from anywhere in the world and to work on their own schedule.
2. Scalability: Drop-shipping makes it easy to scale your business as you can add new products without having to invest in inventory.
3. Minimal risk: Since there's no inventory to manage, drop-shipping minimises the risk of unsold products and lost investment.
4. Easy to test products: Drop-shipping allows retailers to test different products and niches without committing to a large inventory.
5. Access to a wide range of products: Drop-shipping allows retailers to access a wide range of products without having to worry about sourcing, storing, and managing inventory.
6. Lower overhead costs: Drop-shipping retailers don't have to worry about paying for storage space, utilities, and other costs associated with traditional brick-and-mortar retail stores.
7. Focus on sales and marketing.

Drawbacks of Drop-shipping

While drop-shipping offers several advantages, there are also some drawbacks to consider.

1. Low profit margins: Since retailers purchase products at wholesale prices, their profit margins are typically lower than those of traditional retailers.
2. Limited control over inventory: Retailers don't have control over the inventory and fulfilment process, which can lead to issues with product quality and shipping times.
3. Dependence on suppliers: Retailers rely on their suppliers to fulfill orders and handle customer service, which can be a potential risk if the supplier doesn't perform well.
4. Shipping issues: Shipping times can vary depending on the supplier and shipping location, which can lead to delays and customer complaints.
5. Competition: Since drop-shipping has become more popular, there's a lot of competition in the market, which can make it difficult for new retailers to succeed.

Conclusion

Drop-shipping has become an increasingly popular way for entrepreneurs to start an online business with minimal upfront investment. The model allows retailers to sell products without holding inventory, which reduces the risk and cost associated with traditional e-commerce businesses.

There are two main types of drop-shipping: domestic and international. Domestic drop-shipping has the advantage of faster shipping times and lower shipping costs, while international drop-shipping offers a wider range of products and lower wholesale prices.

While drop-shipping offers several benefits, there are also some drawbacks to consider, such as low profit margins and limited control over inventory.

Overall, drop-shipping can be a great way to start an online business, but it's important to do your research and weigh the pros and cons before deciding if it's the right model for you. In the next chapter, we'll explore how to choose a niche and find profitable products to sell in your drop-shipping store.

CHAPTER 2: FINDING PROFITABLE PRODUCTS

If you want to succeed in drop-shipping, finding the right product is crucial. In this chapter, we will discuss how to research profitable product niches, how to source products from reliable suppliers, and provide examples of profitable products to drop-ship.

1, Research profitable product niches

Before you start looking for products to sell, you need to identify profitable product niches. To do this, you need to conduct market research to understand consumer demand, competition, and trends.

a. Use online tools: There are several online tools that you can use to research profitable product niches. One such tool is Google Trends. It allows you to see how often a particular keyword is searched over time, and in different regions. Another tool is Amazon Best Sellers, which shows you the top-selling products in different categories.

b. Identify consumer needs: Look for gaps in the market where consumers have a need that is not being met by existing products. You can do this by browsing online forums, social media groups, and blogs to see what people are talking about.

c. Analyse competition: Look at what your competitors are selling and how they are marketing their products. This will help you understand the demand for certain products and identify gaps in the market.

GOOGLE TRENDS

Here's a step-by-step guide on how to use Google Trends for beginners

1, Go to the Google Trends website: Type in "Google Trends" in your search engine or go directly to the website at www.google.com/trends.

2, Enter your search term: In the search bar at the top of the page, enter a keyword related to the product niche you are researching. For example, if you are interested in selling fitness equipment, you might search for "fitness equipment."

3, Refine your search: Once you have entered your keyword, you can refine your search by location, time period, and category. You can do this by clicking on the various drop-down menus.

4, Analyse the data: The results of your search will be displayed in a graph. The graph shows the interest over time for your keyword. You can see how the interest has changed over time and the regions where the keyword is most popular.

5, Compare search terms: You can also compare the interest in multiple search terms by entering them in the search bar separated by commas. For example, you could compare the interest in "fitness equipment" and "yoga mats" to see which one is more popular.

6, Explore related topics and queries: Below the graph, you will see related topics and related queries. These can give you ideas for related products or keywords that you might want to research.

7, Export the data: If you want to analyze the data further, you can export it to a CSV file by clicking on the "Export" button at the bottom of the page.

Using Google Trends can help you identify profitable product niches by giving you insights into consumer demand and trends over time.

AMAZON BEST SELLERS

Here's a step-by-step guide on how to use Amazon Best Sellers for beginners

1, Go to the Amazon Best Sellers page: Type in "Amazon Best Sellers" in your search engine or go directly to the page at <u>www.amazon.com/Best-Sellers</u>.

2, Select a category: Amazon Best Sellers organises its products by category. Select a category that is relevant to the product niche you are researching. For example, if you are interested in selling pet supplies, select the "Pet Supplies" category.

3, Explore the best sellers: Once you have selected a category, you will see a list of the best-selling products in that category. You can browse through the list to see which products are currently popular.

4, Analyse the product reviews: Click on a product that interests you and scroll down to the product reviews. Read through the reviews to see what customers are saying about the product. Look for any common complaints or issues that customers are experiencing with the product.

5, Look for product opportunities: Based on the information you gather from the best sellers and reviews, look for opportunities to sell similar products. For example, if you notice that a particular type of pet toy is popular, you might want to consider selling similar types of toys.

6, Research the competition: Use Amazon's search bar to look for similar products and check out the competition. Look at the prices, customer reviews, and product descriptions to get an idea of how you can differentiate your products from the competition.

7, Keep an eye on trends: Amazon Best Sellers updates its list hourly, so keep an eye on the list to see how product trends are changing over time.

Using Amazon Best Sellers can help you identify profitable product niches by giving you insights into what products are currently popular and what customers are saying about those products.

By analyzing the best sellers and reviews, you can make informed decisions about the products you want to sell and differentiate your products from the competition.

2, Source products from reliable suppliers

Once you have identified profitable product niches, the next step is to source products from reliable suppliers. Here are some ways to find suppliers:

a. Online directories: Websites like AliExpress, Oberlo, and SaleHoo are online directories of suppliers that you can use to find products to sell.

b. Trade shows: Attend trade shows in your industry to meet with suppliers and see their products in person.

c. Manufacturer websites: Visit the websites of manufacturers that make products in your niche to find contact information for suppliers.

3, Examples of profitable products to drop-ship

a. Health and beauty products: This is a highly profitable niche, as people are always looking for ways to improve their health and appearance. Products like weight loss supplements, skincare products, and vitamins are popular.

b. Pet products: People love their pets, and this is a growing industry. Products like pet food, toys, and accessories are in high demand.

c. Home goods: With more people spending time at home, home goods like furniture, decor, and kitchen gadgets are selling well.

4, Step-by-step strategy

a. Identify profitable niches: Use online tools, analyse competition, and identify consumer needs to find profitable niches.

b. Source products: Use online directories, attend trade shows, and visit manufacturer websites to find reliable suppliers.

c. Analyse profitability: Calculate the profit margin for each product by subtracting the cost of goods sold from the selling price.

d. Test products: Start by listing a few products and testing them to see which ones sell well.

e. Scale up: Once you have identified profitable products, scale up by listing more products and increasing your marketing efforts.

In conclusion, finding profitable products is essential for the success of your drop-shipping business. By researching profitable niches, sourcing products from reliable suppliers, and testing products, you can identify profitable products and scale up your business.

CHAPTER 3: SETTING UP YOUR ONLINE STORE

In this chapter, we will discuss the different options available for building an online store, with a focus on Shopify and other popular store builders.

We will also provide a step-by-step guide on how to set up a Shopify store, including tips for optimising your store for conversions.

Choosing an Online Store Builder

When it comes to building an online store, there are several options available. One popular choice is Shopify, a hosted e-commerce platform that allows you to create an online store quickly and easily.

Other options include WooCommerce, Magento, and BigCommerce, each with their own strengths and weaknesses.

Shopify is a popular choice for beginners because it is easy to use and offers a range of features and templates that allow you to create a professional-looking store quickly. In addition,

Shopify offers a range of integrations with payment gateways, shipping providers, and other third-party apps.

SETTING UP A SHOPIFY STORE

If you decide to use Shopify, here are the steps to set up your store:

Step 1: Sign up for Shopify
To get started, visit the Shopify website and sign up for an account. You will need to enter your email address and create a password to get started.

Step 2: Choose a Theme
Shopify offers a range of templates that you can use to design your store. Choose a theme that fits your brand and style, and customise it as needed.

Step 3: Add Products
Next, you will need to add products to your store. To do this, go to the "Products" tab in your Shopify dashboard and click "Add product." Enter the product name, description, price, and other details, and upload any images or videos you have.

Step 4: Set Up Payment and Shipping
Once you have added your products, you will need to set up payment and shipping options. Shopify integrates with a range of payment gateways, including PayPal, Stripe, and Apple Pay. You can also choose from a range of shipping providers, including USPS, FedEx, and DHL.

Step 5: Customize Your Store
Customize your store by adding pages for policies, FAQs, and other important information. You can also customize your checkout process, add discount codes, and set up email marketing campaigns.

Optimizing Your Store for Conversions

Once your store is up and running, it's important to optimize it for conversions. Here are some tips to help you do this:

1. Use high-quality images and videos to showcase your products.
2. Write compelling product descriptions that highlight the benefits of your products.
3. Make it easy for customers to navigate your store by using clear menus and categories.
4. Use social proof, such as customer reviews, to build trust with potential customers.
5. Offer free shipping or other incentives to encourage customers to make a purchase.
6. Make sure your checkout process is simple and streamlined, with minimal steps required to complete a purchase.

By following these tips and continuously testing and optimizing your store, you can improve your conversion rates and generate more sales.

Here are a few examples of product descriptions:

Fitness Tracker:

Track your fitness goals with our sleek and stylish fitness tracker. With advanced features like heart rate monitoring, sleep tracking, and step counting, you'll be able to stay on top of your health and wellness goals. The durable design and long-lasting battery make this tracker perfect for everyday wear.

Portable Blender:

Make healthy smoothies and shakes on-the-go with our portable blender. This powerful little blender packs a punch, with stainless steel blades and a rechargeable battery. The compact design and easy-to-clean components make it the perfect accessory for your busy lifestyle.

Pet Grooming Kit:

Keep your furry friend looking and feeling their best with our pet grooming kit. This comprehensive kit includes everything you need to groom your pet, including clippers, combs, and brushes. The ergonomic design and quiet operation make it easy to use, and the included carrying case makes it easy to take with you wherever you go.

Smartwatch:

Stay connected and on top of your day with our smartwatch. With features like call and text notifications, GPS tracking, and fitness tracking, this watch is perfect for the busy professional. The sleek design and comfortable fit make it a stylish accessory that can be worn all day.

Electric Toothbrush:

Get a professional-level clean with our electric toothbrush. With multiple cleaning modes and a long-lasting battery, this toothbrush is perfect for anyone who wants to take their oral hygiene to the next level. The compact design and included travel case make it easy to take with you wherever you go.

Here are the pros and cons of the top 5 store builders

Shopify

Pros:

- Easy to use: Shopify is known for its user-friendly interface that allows even beginners to set up their online store quickly and easily.
- Great design templates: The platform offers a wide range of professionally designed templates that can be customised to match your brand identity.
- Large app marketplace: With over 2,500 apps in their app store, Shopify offers a variety of tools and add-ons to help you manage your store more efficiently.

Shopify

Cons:

- Transaction fees if not using Shopify Payments: If you don't use Shopify's in-house payment processing, you'll be charged an additional transaction fee of up to 2%.
- Can be expensive with additional fees: While Shopify's basic plan starts at $29 per month, additional fees can add up quickly, especially if you use a lot of third-party apps.
- Limited control over the design: While Shopify's templates are customizable, there are limits to how much you can change, especially if you're not familiar with coding.

Magento

Pros:

- Scalable and customisable: Magento is known for its flexibility and scalability, making it a popular choice for businesses of all sizes.

- Large user community: With over 250,000 users and a large developer community, Magento has a wealth of resources and support available.

- Powerful features: Magento offers advanced features such as multi-store management, flexible product catalog, and customizable checkout options.

Magento

Cons:

- Expensive to set up and maintain: Magento is one of the most expensive store builders to set up and maintain, requiring specialised hosting, development, and maintenance services.

- Steep learning curve: Due to its complex features, Magento has a steep learning curve, requiring a significant investment of time and resources to master.

- Requires some technical knowledge: Like WooCommerce, Magento requires some technical knowledge of web design and development to get the most out of it.

BigCommerce

Pros:

- All-in-one solution: BigCommerce is an all-in-one solution that includes hosting, security, and support, making it easy for businesses to get up and running quickly.

- User-friendly interface: BigCommerce's user interface is designed for ease of use, making it easy for beginners to set up and manage their store.

- Scalable and flexible: With features like multi-channel selling and customizable templates, BigCommerce can grow with your business.

BigCommerce

Cons:

- Limited customisation: While BigCommerce offers some customisation options, it is not as flexible as other platforms like Magento and WooCommerce.

- Limited app marketplace: With a smaller app marketplace than other platforms, BigCommerce may not offer the variety of tools and add-ons some businesses need.

- Higher pricing: BigCommerce's pricing can be higher than others

Squarespace:

Pros:

- Beautiful, modern templates that are fully customisable

- Offers a wide range of features for e-commerce, including product variants, abandoned cart recovery, and shipping and tax calculators

- Easy-to-use drag and drop interface that doesn't require coding skills

- Provides built-in SEO features to help your store rank higher in search engines

- Offers 24/7 customer support through email and live chat

Squarespace:

Cons:

- Limited customisation options compared to other store builders

- Higher pricing plans than some competitors, with transaction fees on lower-priced plans

- Limited integration options with third-party apps and services

- No built-in multi-language support, requiring third-party plugins or apps

- Limited options for advanced marketing features, such as upselling and cross-selling

WooCommerce

Pros:

- Free to use: WooCommerce is a free plugin for WordPress, making it an affordable option for businesses on a tight budget.

- Full control over the design: As an open-source platform, WooCommerce offers unlimited customization options, from the look and feel of your store to the functionality of your plugins.

- Large user community: With over 5 million active installs, WooCommerce has a large and active user community, making it easy to find resources and support.

WooCommerce

Cons:

- Requires a WordPress website: Unlike other store builders, WooCommerce requires a WordPress website to work, which can add to the setup and maintenance costs.

- Requires some technical knowledge: To get the most out of WooCommerce, you'll need some knowledge of WordPress and web design.

- Limited support: Since WooCommerce is an open-source platform, support is limited to community forums and third-party resources.

WooCommerce

Cons:

- Requires a WordPress website: Unlike other store builders, WooCommerce requires a WordPress website to work, which can add to the setup and maintenance costs.

- Requires some technical knowledge: To get the most out of WooCommerce, you'll need some knowledge of WordPress and web design.

- Limited support: Since WooCommerce is an open-source platform, support is limited to community forums and third-party resources.

Overall, Squarespace is a solid choice for e-commerce stores looking for a beautiful, easy-to-use platform with a good range of features. However, it may not be the best choice for stores looking for extensive customization options or advanced marketing features.

CHAPTER 4: CHOOSING THE RIGHT WHOLESALERS

One of the most important factors in running a successful drop-shipping business is finding reliable and profitable wholesalers.

In this chapter, we'll discuss the different types of wholesalers available, provide a list of reliable and profitable drop-ship wholesalers for beginners, and explain how to evaluate wholesalers based on product selection, pricing, and shipping times.

Types of Wholesalers:

There are several types of wholesalers available to drop-shippers, including:

- Manufacturers - These are companies that produce products directly, and often offer the best pricing for dropshippers. However, they may require large minimum order quantities (MOQs).

- Distributors - These are companies that buy products in bulk from manufacturers and then sell them to retailers or dropshippers. They offer a wider selection of products and may have lower MOQs than manufacturers.

- Aggregators - These are companies that collect products from multiple manufacturers and distributors, and then sell them to dropshippers. They offer a wide range of products from different suppliers, but may have higher prices than manufacturers or distributors.

Here are some reliable and profitable drop-ship wholesalers for beginners:

1. AliExpress - This is a popular platform that connects buyers with Chinese manufacturers and distributors. It offers a wide range of products at competitive prices, but shipping times can be longer.
2. Doba - This is an aggregator that offers products from multiple suppliers. It provides a wide range of products and a user-friendly interface, but has higher prices and fees than other platforms.
3. SaleHoo - This is a directory of wholesalers and manufacturers, providing access to over 8,000 suppliers. It offers a wide range of products and a good selection of features, but may require additional fees for certain services.
4. Oberlo - This is a drop-shipping platform that integrates with Shopify. It offers a user-friendly interface and a wide range of products, but has limited customisation options.
5. Spocket - This is a drop-shipping platform that offers products from suppliers in the US and Europe. It provides fast shipping times and a good selection of products, but may have higher prices than other platforms.

Evaluating Wholesalers:

When evaluating wholesalers, it's important to consider several factors, including:

- Product Selection - Look for wholesalers with a wide range of products that fit your niche and target audience.

- Pricing - Compare prices from different wholesalers to find the best deals, but be aware of hidden fees or minimum order quantities.

- Shipping Times - Consider the shipping times offered by the wholesaler, as longer shipping times may lead to lower customer satisfaction.

- Reputation - Check reviews and ratings of the wholesaler to ensure they have a good reputation and reliable customer service.

- Policies - Read the wholesaler's policies on returns, refunds, and warranties to ensure they align with your own policies.

Examples:

Let's say you're starting a dropshipping business selling pet products. After researching different wholesalers, you decide to use Spocket and SaleHoo.

Spocket offers a wide range of pet products with fast shipping times from suppliers in the US and Europe. SaleHoo provides access to over 8,000 suppliers with a good selection of pet products at competitive prices.

To evaluate these wholesalers, you compare their pricing for similar products and read reviews from other dropshippers. You find that Spocket has slightly higher prices but faster shipping times, while SaleHoo offers lower prices but longer shipping times from overseas suppliers.

Ultimately, you decide to use both wholesalers to diversify your product selection and offer faster shipping times for some products.

Here's a step-by-step guide on how to contact dropship wholesalers and start working with them:

- Research potential wholesalers: Use resources such as SaleHoo, Worldwide Brands, or Google to find potential wholesalers that offer products in your niche.

- Evaluate wholesalers: Once you have a list of potential wholesalers, evaluate each one based on criteria such as product selection, pricing, shipping times, and customer service. You can also check online reviews and ratings to get an idea of their reputation.

- Contact the wholesaler: Once you have identified a few promising wholesalers, reach out to them to inquire about their dropshipping program. You can usually find their contact information on their website, or you can use a contact form or email address.

- Introduce yourself: In your initial contact, introduce yourself and explain that you are interested in dropshipping their products. Be professional and polite in your communication.

- Ask about their dropshipping program: Ask the wholesaler about their dropshipping program and any requirements they may have. Some wholesalers may require an application or approval process before you can start dropshipping their products.

- Request product and pricing information: Ask the wholesaler for product and pricing information, including wholesale prices, shipping costs, and any other fees or minimum order requirements.

- Negotiate terms: If you are satisfied with the wholesaler's products and pricing, you can negotiate the terms of your agreement, such as profit margins and payment terms.

- Start dropshipping: Once you have agreed on the terms with the wholesaler, you can start listing their products on your online store and fulfill orders as they come in.

It's important to remember that building a strong relationship with your wholesaler is key to your success as a dropshipper.

Maintain open and honest communication, fulfill orders promptly, and address any issues that arise in a timely manner. This will help you build a positive reputation with your customers and your wholesaler.

CHAPTER 5: MARKETING YOUR DROP-SHIPPING BUSINESS

Congratulations! You have set up your drop-shipping store and now it's time to promote it.

Marketing your drops=hipping business is crucial to increase your sales and revenue.

In this chapter, we will discuss various marketing strategies and provide examples of successful drops-hipping businesses.

Social Media Marketing:

Social media is a powerful tool to promote your business. It's important to identify which social media platforms are best suited for your business. Here are some popular social media platforms and tips on how to use them effectively:

- Facebook: Create a business page, post engaging content, and run Facebook ads targeting your audience. Use Facebook insights to track your performance.

- Instagram: Post visually appealing images and videos of your products. Use hashtags to increase visibility and collaborate with influencers to reach a wider audience.

- Twitter: Tweet about your products and engage with your followers. Use Twitter ads to promote your business.

Email Marketing:

Email marketing is an effective way to keep your customers engaged and informed about your products. Here are some tips on how to use email marketing effectively:

- Build an email list: Encourage visitors to sign up for your newsletter by offering a discount or free product.

- Send targeted emails: Segment your email list based on their interests and behaviour. Send personalised emails with product recommendations.

- Use catchy subject lines: Your subject line should be catchy and relevant to your email content.

Email marketing is the process of sending promotional messages or newsletters to a list of subscribers via email. This marketing technique allows businesses to engage with their customers and prospects by sending them targeted messages directly to their inbox.

Here are the steps to create a successful email marketing campaign:

- Build your email list: The first step in email marketing is to create an email list of subscribers who have opted in to receive your emails. You can build your list by offering a sign-up form on your website or by asking customers to provide their email address at checkout.

- Choose an email marketing service: There are several email marketing services available, such as Mailchimp, Constant Contact, and Campaign Monitor. Choose the one that suits your needs, sign up and import your email list.

- Create a targeted message: Your email should be personalised and tailored to the interests of your subscribers. Consider segmenting your email list based on demographics, behaviour, or interests, and create different messages for each segment.

- Craft a compelling subject line: Your subject line should grab the reader's attention and entice them to open your email. Avoid using spammy or click-bait subject lines.

- Design your email: Use a professional email template and include engaging images and clear call-to-action buttons.

- Send your email: Schedule your email to send at a time when your subscribers are most likely to check their inbox. You can also set up automated emails to send at specific intervals.

- Analyze your results: Track the success of your email campaign by analyzing the open and click-through rates. Use this information to improve your future email campaigns.

Email marketing can be an effective way to reach your target audience and build long-term relationships with your customers. By following these steps and using best practices, you can create successful email campaigns that drive conversions and grow your business.

Advertising:

Advertising is a great way to increase your visibility and reach a wider audience. Here are some popular advertising platforms:

- Google Ads: Create targeted ads based on keywords and demographics.

- Facebook Ads: Run ads targeting your audience based on interests, behavior, and location.

- Influencer marketing: Collaborate with influencers who have a large following on social media platforms.

Google Ads is an advertising platform that allows businesses to display their ads on Google search results pages, other Google-owned platforms such as YouTube and Gmail, and on third-party websites that participate in the Google Display Network.

Setting up a Google Ads campaign can be done in a few simple steps:

- Create a Google Ads account: To create an account, go to the Google Ads website and click on the "Start Now" button. You'll be asked to enter your email address and website URL to get started.

- Choose your campaign type: Google Ads offers a variety of campaign types, including search, display, shopping, and video campaigns. Choose the campaign type that best suits your business goals.

- Set your budget: Decide how much you want to spend on your campaign each day. Google Ads allows you to set a daily budget and will automatically stop showing your ads once your budget is exhausted.

- Select your target audience: Choose who you want to show your ads to. You can target specific locations, languages, demographics, interests, and behaviors.

- Create your ad groups: Ad groups are sets of ads and keywords that are organized around a specific theme. Create ad groups that are relevant to your products or services.

- Write your ads: Write compelling ads that are relevant to your ad groups and include your targeted keywords.

- Choose your keywords: Keywords are the words or phrases that people use to search for products or services on Google. Choose relevant keywords that match your ad groups and write ads that incorporate those keywords.

- Set up conversion tracking: Conversion tracking allows you to track how many people are clicking on your ads and taking action on your website, such as making a purchase or filling out a form.

- Launch your campaign: Once you've set up your campaign, review your settings and launch your ads. Monitor your campaign performance regularly and make adjustments as needed to improve your results.

Facebook Ads is a popular advertising platform that allows businesses to create and run ads to reach their target audience on Facebook and its related platforms, including Instagram, Messenger, and Audience Network.

- To create a Facebook ad, you first need to have a Facebook Business Manager account. From there, you can select the "Create" button in the Ads Manager section to start building your ad campaign.

- The first step is to choose your campaign objective, such as increasing brand awareness or driving sales. Then, you can select your target audience based on factors like demographics, interests, and behaviours. You can also choose your ad placement, ad format, and budget.

- When creating your ad, you'll need to choose from different ad formats, such as image, video, carousel, or collection. You can also add a headline, ad copy, and call-to-action button to encourage people to take action.

- Once your ad is created and approved by Facebook, it will be displayed to your target audience in their newsfeed or other designated locations. You can track the performance of your ads and adjust your targeting or budget as needed.

Overall, Facebook Ads can be a powerful tool for reaching your target audience and driving traffic and sales to your dropshipping business. However, it's important to have a clear strategy and understanding of your target audience in order to make the most of your ad spend.

Building Your Brand Identity:

Creating a strong brand identity is important for the success of your drop-shipping business. Here are some tips on how to build your brand:

- Develop a brand voice and tone: Define your brand voice and tone and use it consistently across all your marketing channels.

- Create a logo and tagline: Your logo and tagline should be memorable and relevant to your brand.

- Use high-quality images: Use high-quality images of your products on your website and social media platforms.

Examples of Successful Dropshipping Businesses:

Here are some successful drop-shipping businesses and their marketing strategies:

- Gymshark: Gymshark uses influencer marketing on social media platforms like Instagram to promote their fitness apparel.

- MVMT Watches: MVMT Watches uses Facebook ads to promote their stylish watches.

- Hubble: Hubble uses email marketing to promote their affordable and stylish contact lenses.

By implementing these marketing strategies and building a strong brand identity, you can increase your sales and revenue and make your drop-shipping business successful.

CHAPTER 6: MANAGING YOUR DROPSHIPPING BUSINESS

Managing a dropshipping business can be challenging, especially as it grows and scales.

In this chapter, we will discuss the key aspects of managing a successful dropshipping business, including inventory management, customer service, and scaling for growth.

Inventory Management

One of the most critical aspects of a drop-shipping business is managing your inventory effectively. As a dropshipper, you are entirely reliant on your suppliers to provide the products that your customers order. Therefore, it's essential to have a system in place that allows you to track inventory levels and stay up-to-date with product availability.

There are many different inventory management systems available that can help you streamline this process. Many of these systems will automatically update your inventory levels based on sales, alert you when stock levels are low, and even reorder products automatically when necessary.

Inventory management is a critical component of a successful drop-shipping business. Without a proper system in place, you may face stock-outs, overstocks, and unhappy customers. Here are some examples of inventory management systems that you can use for your drop-shipping business:

- Shopify: Shopify offers an easy-to-use inventory management system that is integrated with your store. With Shopify, you can track your inventory levels, receive low stock alerts, and set up automated inventory tracking for your products. You can also create product bundles and manage your stock levels for each variant.

- TradeGecko: TradeGecko is a cloud-based inventory management software that can help you manage your stock levels, sales, and purchasing. With TradeGecko, you can create purchase orders, track your inventory levels in real-time, and manage multiple warehouses. You can also generate reports on your sales, purchases, and inventory levels.

- Zoho Inventory: Zoho Inventory is another cloud-based inventory management software that can help you track your inventory levels, orders, and shipping. With Zoho Inventory, you can manage your sales channels, purchase orders, and track your stock levels across multiple warehouses. You can also automate your order fulfilment process and generate reports on your sales and inventory levels.

- ShipBob: ShipBob is a fulfillment and inventory management service that can help you manage your inventory levels, shipping, and returns. With ShipBob, you can store your products in their warehouses, manage your inventory levels, and automate your order fulfillment process. You can also track your orders in real-time and receive alerts when your stock levels are low.

- Skubana: Skubana is an all-in-one inventory management software that can help you manage your inventory levels, sales channels, and orders. With Skubana, you can track your inventory levels in real-time, manage your sales channels, and automate your order fulfillment process. You can also generate reports on your sales, purchases, and inventory levels.

These inventory management systems can help you streamline your drop-shipping business and ensure that you always have the right products in stock. Choose the system that best fits your needs and budget, and start managing your inventory like a pro!

Customer Service

Providing excellent customer service is critical to the success of any business, and drop-shipping is no exception. As a drop-shipper, you may not have physical control over the products you sell, but you are still responsible for ensuring that your customers receive their orders in a timely and satisfactory manner.

One way to provide excellent customer service is to communicate with your customers regularly. Keep them informed of their order status, provide tracking information, and address any concerns or issues they may have promptly.

Another critical aspect of customer service is handling returns and refunds. It's essential to have clear policies in place and to communicate these policies to your customers upfront.

Make the return process as easy and straightforward as possible, and always strive to resolve any issues quickly and to your customer's satisfaction.

Scaling for Growth

As your drop-shipping business grows, you will need to develop strategies for scaling your operations to meet demand. This may include hiring additional staff, expanding your product line, or investing in new technology to streamline your processes.

One critical aspect of scaling your drop-shipping business is managing your cash flow effectively. You will need to reinvest profits into your business to fuel growth, but you must also manage expenses carefully to ensure that you are not overspending.

Another critical factor in scaling your drop-shipping business is building strong relationships with your suppliers. As you grow, you will likely need to negotiate better pricing and terms with your suppliers to remain competitive. Building a strong relationship with your suppliers can help you secure better deals and ensure that you have the products you need to meet demand.

Conclusion

After reading this book, we hope that you have gained a better understanding of what it takes to start a successful dropshipping business. You've learned about the basics of dropshipping, how to research profitable products and source reliable suppliers, and how to set up an online store using different store builders. We also covered how to market your business through various channels and manage your inventory and growth.

It's important to remember that starting a drop-shipping business is not a get-rich-quick scheme, but rather a long-term investment. It takes time and effort to build a successful business, but with the right strategy and dedication, you can create a passive income stream.

We encourage you to take action and apply the knowledge you have gained in this book. Find a profitable niche, source reliable suppliers, set up your online store, and start marketing your business. Remember to focus on providing excellent customer service and optimizing your store for conversions.

Successful examples of dropshipping businesses:

- Gymshark - a fitness apparel brand that started as a dropshipping business and has now grown to become a multi-million dollar company.
- MVMT - a watch and accessories brand that began as a dropshipping business and now has a large following and several retail stores.
- Hubble Contacts - an online contact lens retailer that uses a dropshipping model to offer affordable, high-quality lenses.
- Spocket - a dropshipping platform that connects online retailers with suppliers to offer fast and reliable shipping times.
- Inkthreadable - a UK-based print-on-demand dropshipping company that specializes in custom clothing and accessories.

These businesses have all found success by leveraging the benefits of dropshipping, including low overhead costs, flexibility, and the ability to offer a wide range of products without holding inventory. They have also focused on creating strong brands, providing excellent customer service, and utilizing effective marketing strategies to reach their target audiences.

Here are a few more examples of successful dropshipping businesses and their marketing strategies:

- Gymshark: Gymshark started out as a drop-shipping business in 2012 and has since grown into a multi-million dollar brand. Their marketing strategy includes using social media influencers to promote their products, creating a strong brand image, and hosting events to engage with their audience.

- MVMT: MVMT is a watch brand that started as a dropshipping business in 2013. Their marketing strategy includes using Facebook and Instagram ads to target their audience, creating engaging content on social media, and partnering with other brands and influencers.

- Wayfair: Wayfair is an online home goods retailer that utilizes a dropshipping model. Their marketing strategy includes creating a user-friendly website, offering competitive pricing, and providing excellent customer service.

- ColourPop: ColourPop is a makeup brand that began as a dropshipping business in 2014. Their marketing strategy includes using Instagram and YouTube influencers to promote their products, offering limited edition releases to create hype, and providing high-quality products at an affordable price.

- Zenni Optical: Zenni Optical is an online eyewear retailer that utilizes a dropshipping model. Their marketing strategy includes using search engine optimization (SEO) to drive traffic to their website, offering a wide variety of affordable products, and providing excellent customer service.

Overall, these successful dropshipping businesses utilized various marketing strategies such as social media influencer marketing, targeted advertising, creating a strong brand image, providing excellent customer service, and offering competitive pricing to drive their success.

If you need further support or want to learn more, we have provided additional resources at the end of this book. Thank you for reading, and we wish you the best of luck in your dropshipping journey.

here are some additional resources for readers interested in learning more about drop-shipping:

- Oberlo Blog: Oberlo is a popular app used for drop=shipping on Shopify. Their blog provides tips and advice on drop-shipping, as well as success stories from entrepreneurs.

- eComElites: A comprehensive drop-shipping course by Franklin Hatchett that covers everything from niche research to marketing strategies.

- Drop-ship Lifestyle: A popular drop-shipping course by Anton Kraly that includes training videos, live webinars, and a community forum.

- Reddit: The r/dropship subreddit is a great place to ask questions, share advice, and connect with other drop-shippers.

- eCommerceFuel: A community of eCommerce entrepreneurs that provides resources, advice, and networking opportunities.

- Google Ads Help Center: A comprehensive guide to setting up and running Google Ads campaigns.

- Facebook Business Help Center: A resource for learning how to set up and manage Facebook ads.

- Email Marketing Best Practices: A guide to creating effective email marketing campaigns.

- Shopify Academy: A collection of free courses and resources for entrepreneurs looking to start or grow their online businesses.

- Alibaba: A popular sourcing website for finding reliable wholesalers and manufacturers.

These resources should provide readers with additional information and support as they begin their dropshipping journey.

www.ingramcontent.com/pod-product-compliance
Lightning Source LLC
Chambersburg PA
CBHW070457220526
45466CB00004B/1865